# BEER

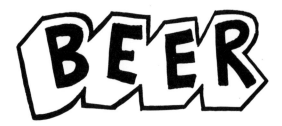

# BEER

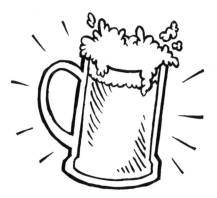

## MAKES DADDY STRONG

**CHRONICLE BOOKS**
SAN FRANCISCO

First published in the United States in 2013 by Chronicle Books.

First Published in the United Kingdom in 2011 by Hodder & Stoughton,
an Hachette UK company.

Text and illustrations copyright
© 2013 by Andy Riley.

Library of Congress Cataloging-in-Publication Data

Riley, Andy.
  Beer makes daddy strong / Andy Riley.
    p. cm.
  ISBN 978-1-4521-1208-4
  1.  English wit and humor, Pictorial. 2.  Fathers--Caricatures and
cartoons. 3.  Fatherhood--Caricatures and cartoons.  I. Title.

  NC1479.R55A4 2013b
  741.5'6941--dc23

                              2012026429

Manufactured in China.

10 9 8 7 6 5 4 3

Chronicle Books, LLC
680 Second Street
San Francisco, California 94107
www.chroniclebooks.com

ANDY RILEY IS THE AUTHOR/ARTIST OF THE BOOK OF BUNNY SUICIDES, DAWN OF THE BUNNY SUICIDES AND EVERY OTHER BUNNY SUICIDE THING. HIS OTHER BOOKS INCLUDE GREAT LIES TO TELL SMALL KIDS, LOADS MORE LIES TO TELL SMALL KIDS, SELFISH PIGS, ROASTED AND D.I.Y. DENTISTRY.

HIS SCRIPTWRITING WORK INCLUDES BLACK BOOKS, THE GREAT OUTDOORS, HYPERDRIVE, LITTLE BRITAIN, ARMSTRONG AND MILLER, GNOMEO & JULIET, THE ARMANDO IANNUCCI SHOWS, HARRY+PAUL, SLACKER CATS AND THE BAFTA-WINNING ANIMATION ROBBIE THE REINDEER.

misterandyriley.com

WITH THANKS TO:
GORDON WISE, LISA HIGHTON,
POLLY FABER AND KEVIN CECIL.

# CAR GAMES


OKAY
LET'S PLAY "WHO CAN STAY QUIET THE LONGEST"

DADDY KNOWS
LOTS OF GOOD ONES

# MAN
# FLU

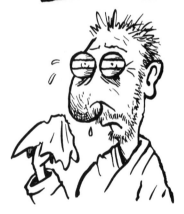

DADDY WOULD RATHER
YOU DIDN'T LAUGH
AT IT

# FRIES

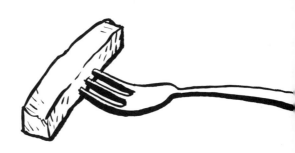

ARE WHAT DAD
STEALS OFF YOUR
PLATE WHEN HE
SAID HE DIDN'T
WANT ANY

# "WHO'S THE DADDY?"

IS WHAT DADDY
LIKES TO SAY SOMETIMES

IT'S PROBABLY FROM
A FILM OR SOMETHING

IT MAKES HIM HAPPY, ANYWAY

# THE INTERESTING ARTICLE <u>NEXT</u> TO THE BREASTS

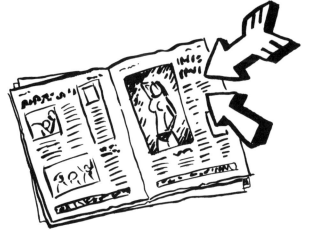

<u>THAT'S</u> WHAT DADDY'S LOOKING AT

# CONVERSATIONS WITH DAD

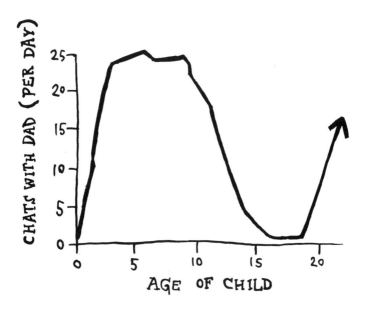

THEY WILL RETURN,
IN THE END

# SILLY HATS AT ROCK FESTIVALS

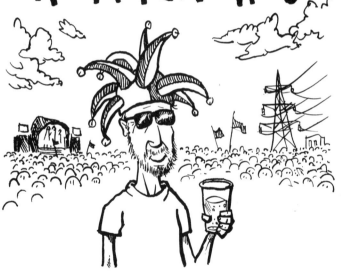

WHO SAYS DAD'S
TOO OLD FOR THEM?

# KITE

IF YOU CAN'T GET IT IN THE AIR YOU WON'T FEEL LIKE A PROPER DAD

# A NEW PHONE

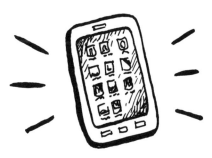

DADDY REALLY
REALLY WANTS ONE

ABOUT 2 WEEKS AFTER
HE GOT THE LAST ONE

# THE "FLOORDROBE"

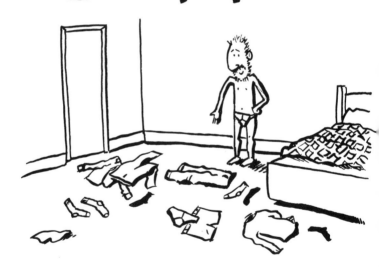

DADDY SAYS HE
PIONEERED THE CONCEPT

# SPEED CAMERAS


!!
$20
$20

DADDY'S GOT SOME OPINIONS

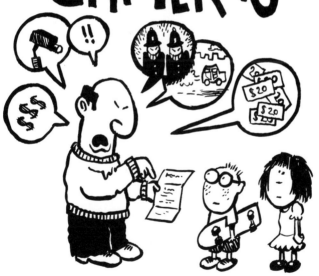

# THOSE COLORFUL TIES

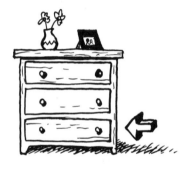

THAT YOU BOUGHT FOR
DADDY ON PREVIOUS FATHERS'
DAYS ARE KEPT IN A
SPECIAL DRAWER

SO SPECIAL IN FACT

THAT THEY NEVER
COME OUT
OF IT

# TOY STORY 3

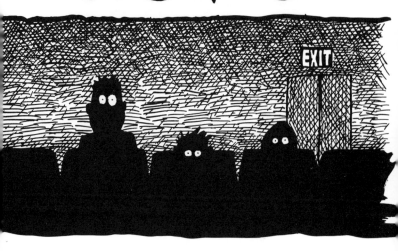

IT WAS NICE AND
DARK IN THE CINEMA

SO NO ONE SAW
DADDY CRY

# SPAGHETTI BOLOGNESE

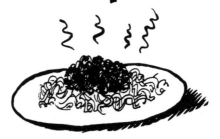

DAD COOKS A GREAT ONE

GOOD JOB TOO CAUSE IT'S ABOUT
THE ONLY THING HE **CAN** COOK

SO IF YOU DON'T
LIKE IT — TOUGH

# TREE
# HOUSES

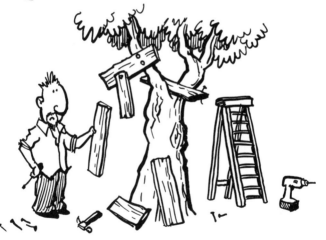

OF *COURSE*
DADDY KNOWS HOW
TO BUILD ONE

# MODEL PLANES

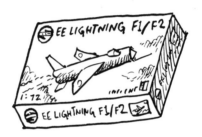

MAKE DADDY NOSTALGIC
WHEN HE SEES THEM
IN SHOPS

BUT HE DOESN'T ACTUALLY
WANT TO *BUILD* ONE ANY
TIME SOON SO DON'T
BUY HIM ONE
FOR HIS BIRTHDAY

# DIVING BOARDS

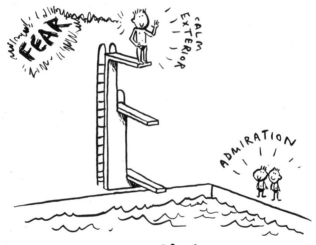

A DAD ALWAYS HAS TO
PROVE HE CAN
JUMP OFF THE
HIGHEST ONE

# THE BOUNCY CASTLE

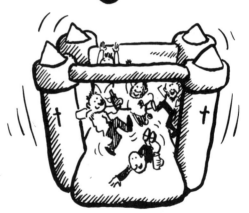

DADDY LIKES A GO ON IT AT THE END OF THE KIDS' PARTY

ALONG WITH THE OTHER DADDIES

# STITCHES

DADDY GOT THREE
OF THEM AFTER HE
BOUNCED OUT OF
THE BOUNCY CASTLE

HE DOESN'T LIKE TO
TALK ABOUT IT

# THE CAMPING TRIP

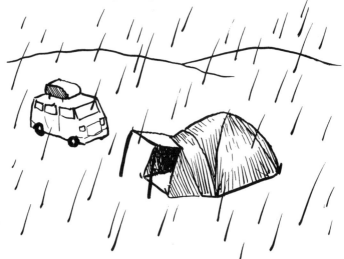

WAS DEFINITELY
DADDY'S IDEA

THAT'S WHAT MOMMY
KEEPS SAYING ANYWAY

# AN *INCURABLE ROMANTIC*

.... SOMETIMES DADDY REMEMBERS TO BE ONE ( ONCE EVERY COUPLE OF YEARS)

# SPICY FOODS



DADDY'S GOT TO PRETEND HE ENJOYS THEM

IT'S PART OF BEING A MAN

# DADDY PRIDE

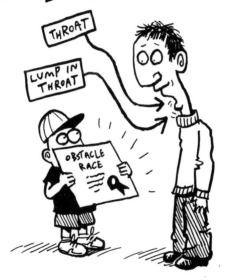

YOU NEVER KNOW
WHEN IT'S GOING
TO HIT

# THE SUPER BOWL


FACT
FACT
FACT

TURNS DADDY INTO A FOOTBALL EXPERT

ONCE EVERY YEAR

# MIDLIFE CRISIS CARS

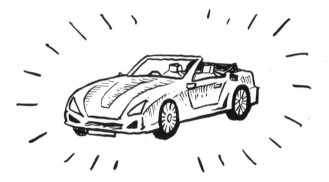

DADDY KNOWS
THEY'RE STUPID

BUT HE WANTS
ONE ANYWAY

# DADDY'S OLD VINYL


LAST PLAYED 1995
LAST PLAYED 1999

SOMEHOW

DADDY CAN'T BRING HIMSELF TO THROW IT AWAY

# SCARS


AND I GOT THIS ONE RUNNING WITH THE BULLS IN PAMPLONA*
WOW

DAD LOVES TO SHOW THEM OFF

(*LIE)

# MAP-READING


...TURN RIGHT.
ONLY IF I WANT TO
MY CAR, MY RULES

A PRIME "DADDY SKILL"

NOW MADE IRRELEVANT BY GPS TECHNOLOGY

# THE DVD OF MAMMA MIA


OOH! LET'S WATCH THIS AGAIN
MAMMA MIA

OTHERWISE KNOWN AS
"DADDY KRYPTONITE"

# "THE MOVES"

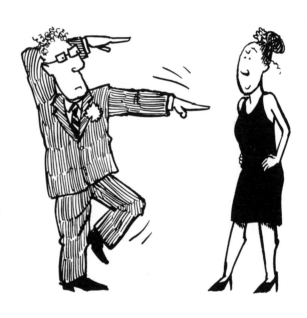

DADDY'S STILL GOT THEM
THEY MOSTLY COME
OUT AT WEDDINGS

# TRIUMPH

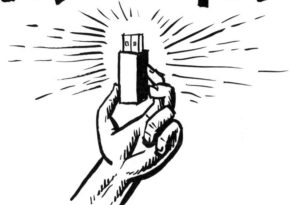

THE FEELING DADDY GETS WHEN
HE FINDS A MEMORY STICK
CONTAINING THE FIRST TWO YEARS
OF CHILD PHOTOS, THOUGHT LOST
WHEN THE COMPUTER DIED

MIXED IN WITH A BIT OF RELIEF

CAUSE MOMMY WON'T KILL HIM NOW

# WALKING THE DOG

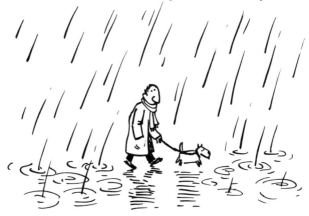

ALWAYS SEEMS TO
BE DADDY'S JOB
WHEN IT'S RAINING

# VENN DIAGRAMS

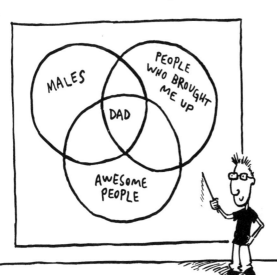

...MAKE EVERYTHING CLEAR

# WWII DOCUMENTARIES

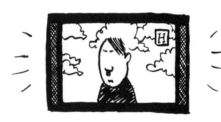

DAD CAN WATCH
THREE IN A ROW

# GOING TO THE DUMP

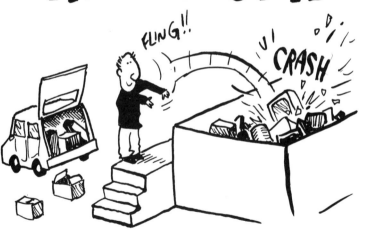

DADDY PRETENDS IT'S A CHORE
BUT REALLY IT'S ONE OF
HIS FAVORITE THINGS

# SHOPPING

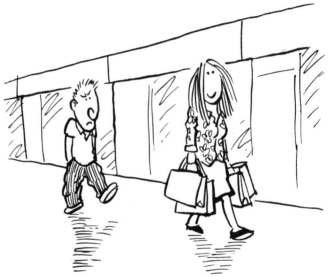

IS NOT SOMETHING DADDY REGARDS AS A LEISURE ACTIVITY IN ITS OWN RIGHT

# DAD'S TAXI CO.

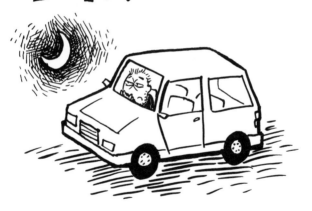

- 24 HOURS A DAY
- 365 DAYS A YEAR

# SUNDAY PAPERS



DAD?
DAD
DA-AA-
-AAAD...


GIVE DAD A
GREAT PLACE
TO HIDE

# THE
# Wii

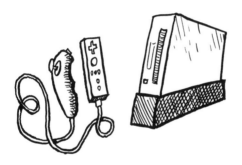

DADDY BOUGHT IT
"FOR THE KIDS"

YEAH, RIGHT

# PORK RINDS

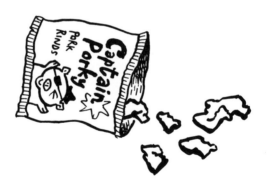

TWO PINTS IN,
AND DADDY CAN'T
RESIST THEM

# POWERPOINT


TIDYING UP
• FUN
• HELPFUL
• 'COOL'

DAD MIGHT START USING IT AT HOME AS WELL AS WORK

# GARDENING:

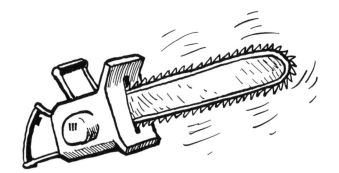

- MOMMY PLANTS STUFF
- DADDY **CHOPS IT BACK**

# PARENTS' EVENINGS

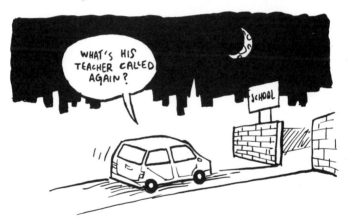

# DAD ALWAYS PUTS IN THE RESEARCH

# $800 FOR A HANDBAG



DADDY WILL NEVER UNDERSTAND ***THAT***

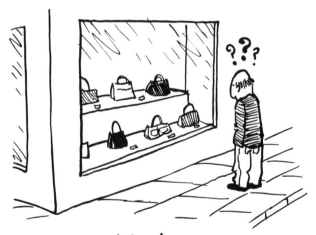

# SHOULDER RIDES

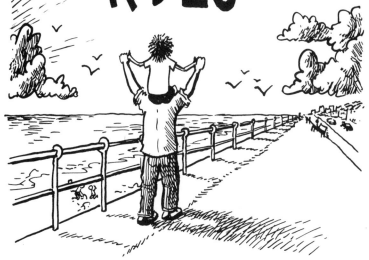

ALWAYS WERE A
MAGICAL MOMENT
WITH
DAD

# DADDY'S HAIR

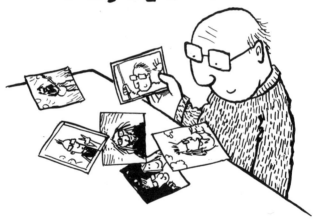

THE PHOTOGRAPHS
HELP HIM REMEMBER

# THE BARBECUE

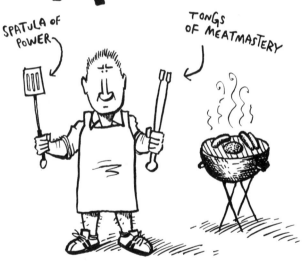

SPATULA OF POWER

TONGS OF MEATMASTERY

....DADDY'S DOMAIN

# SURVIVING IN THE WILD

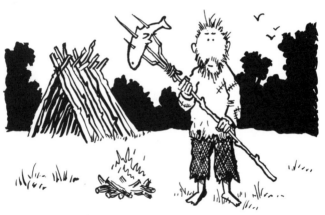

DADDY KNOWS HE'D BE VERY
GOOD AT IT BECAUSE HE'S
WATCHED A *LOT* OF TV
ABOUT IT

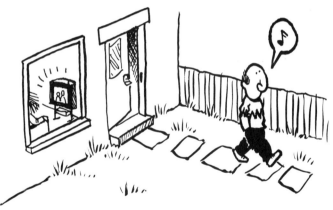

# THE BACHELOR IS ON

SUDDENLY, DAD
THINKS OF SOMETHING
IMPORTANT TO DO
SOMEWHERE ELSE

# AT THE DENTIST

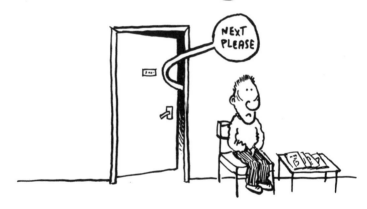

THE ONLY TIME
DADDY SHOWS FEAR

# THE 5K
## CHARITY FUN RUN

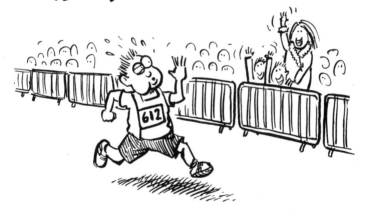

IT'S NOT A MARATHON
BUT IT STILL MAKES DADDY
A **HERO**

# SHOUTING ON THE SIDELINE


GO ON SON
RAKE YOUR CLEATS DOWN HIS LEG
JUST LIKE WE PRACTICED

DADDY'S PROMISED NOT TO DO IT AGAIN

# GRAND CHILDREN

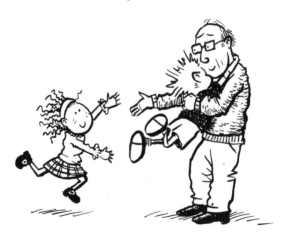

MAKE DADDY PROUD
ALL OVER AGAIN

# THE WEDDING ANNIVERSARY

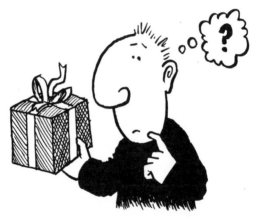

ONE DAY, SOMEONE WILL EXPLAIN TO DADDY WHY IT'S ALWAYS THE MAN'S JOB TO REMEMBER IT

AND

AND!!

WE LOVE DAD
THIS MUCH

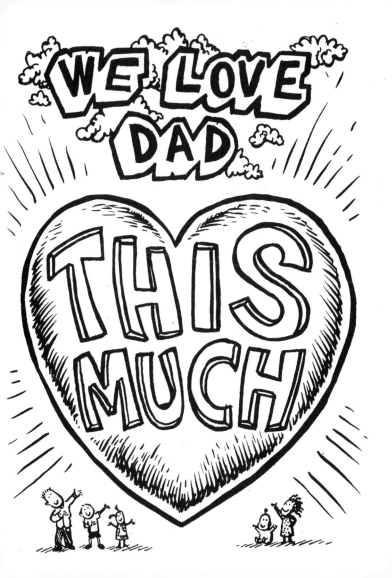

REFILL
REQUIRED

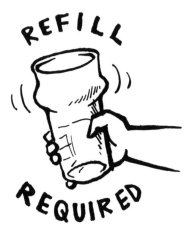